I0450041

LEGAL NOTICE

The Author does not warrant the accuracy, completeness or currency of this publication. In particular, the Author does not warrant or represent at any time that the contents within are accurate due to the rapidly changing nature of the business.

While all attempts have been made to verify information provided in this publication, the Author assumes no responsibility for errors, omissions, or contrary interpretation of the subject matter herein. Any perceived slights of specific persons, peoples, or organizations are unintentional.

This book is a common sense guide to advertising and design. In practical advice books, like anything else in life, there are no guarantees of income made. Readers are cautioned to reply on their own judgment about their individual circumstances to act accordingly.

This book is not intended for use as a source of legal, business, accounting or financial advice. All readers are advised to seek services of competent professionals in legal, business, accounting, and finance field. The Author disclaims all liability with respect to the results of any actions taken or not taken in reliance upon this publication.

© Copyright 2006 Jamie Hardie
All rights reserved. No part of this publication may be reproduced, stored in a retrieval system, or transmitted, in any form or by any means, electronic, mechanical, photocopying, recording, or otherwise, without the written prior permission of the author.

Note for Librarians: A cataloguing record for this book is available from Library and Archives Canada at www.collectionscanada.ca/amicus/index-e.html
ISBN 1-4251-0644-7

Printed on paper with minimum 30% recycled fibre.
Trafford's print shop runs on "green energy" from solar, wind and other environmentally-friendly power sources.

PUBLISHING™
Offices in Canada, USA, Ireland and UK

Book sales for North America and international:
Trafford Publishing, 6E–2333 Government St.,
Victoria, BC V8T 4P4 CANADA
phone 250 383 6864 (toll-free 1 888 232 4444)
fax 250 383 6804; email to orders@trafford.com
Book sales in Europe:
Trafford Publishing (UK) Limited, 9 Park End Street, 2nd Floor
Oxford, UK OX1 1HH UNITED KINGDOM
phone +44 (0)1865 722 113 (local rate 0845 230 9601)
facsimile +44 (0)1865 722 868; info.uk@trafford.com
Order online at:
trafford.com/06-2402

10 9 8 7 6 5 4 3 2

What others are saying...

This is truly is a great little reference book.
I read a lot of these and in my opinion it is one of the best."
Wayne Myers
Marketing Manager, *Plant Products Company Ltd.*

"*Get Noticed* is exactly what I find most useful. Short,
concise and to the point. Easy to read on a plane, at the
airport or between meetings, highlighting useful points
that I can quickly put into action.

"*Get Noticed* is a valuable and informative book.
I thoroughly enjoyed it, and reinforces why you are so
good at what you do!" "Well done!"
Darryl Culley
President, *Emergency Management & Training Inc.*

Clearly laid-out and cleverly written, this book does what it
says it will do! With dashes of humor sprinkled throughout,
Hardie not only draws from a wide range of design principles, but he goes far beyond that by concisely explaining
how YOU can achieve amazing results for YOUR own small
business. A refreshing read!
Christine Crawley
Graphic Designer, *CCgraphics*

What others are saying...

"This book reminds us to go back to basics and to be true to the desired outcome. A highly recommended piece of work!"
Debbie Brown
Owner, Browns Craft

"Best damned book about advertising strategies for small business that I have come across... ever!"
Howard Murray
President, *Firestorm Turbines Inc.*

"I love that you have put so many valuable advertising and marketing tips into an easily digestible format."
Barbara Stuhlemmer
President, *ClearComm Information Design*

"I can't believe it ... it's like you've read our collective minds"
Carole
Newmarket, ON

"Hardie and Company provide us with a personal attention to detail that ultimately reflects our organizational philosophy. Over many years we have <u>never</u> been disappointed!"
Sandy Milakovic
Executive Director, *Canadian Mental Health Association Peel*

What others are saying...

"Never mind 5 minutes to read small bits. "*Get Noticed*" beckons you to carry on for more info! At the end you'll think, that's all doable. A concise, loaded guide. A resourceful reference book, bulging with tried true practices that are simple to conceptualize."

"Hardie and Company did an exceptional job in producing an ad to assist us in penetrating the Middle East market. Not only was the final product spectacular, but they worked with, and supported us each step of the way from consultation to final product. "

Tony da Silva
Director, *Centre for Education and Training*

"A major concern for our company is being able to access innovative marketing ideas that get attention and cut costs. Hardie & Co... helps us do that — good, practical advice when needed most. "

Wayne Myers
Product Marketing Manager, *Plant Products Co. Ltd.*

© Hardie & Co. - All rights reserved   www.hardieandcompany.com   3

What others are saying...

"Jamie took the time to learn about, and to care about what we do; finding creative solutions to obstacles, so that the final result would be excellent, not just 'good' enough'. We are delighted!"

Jack Fleming
North Peel & Dufferin, *Community Legal Services*

"We've NEVER had results like this from our advertising in the past.
Their personal involvement in learning our business enabled them to present our product with a level of detail and enthusiasm that would make you think they were our neighbours! They knew exactly what would work best for us and our market!"

Howard Murray
President, *Firestorm Turbines Inc.*

"This book is full of "Ah-ha!" moments...it really shows you the common sense basics of advertising for a small business."

Cathy White
Educator

"Simply refreshing!"

© Hardie & Co. - All rights reserved
www.hardieandcompany.com

Table of Contents

"What's in it for me?"

O kay, you've spent good money for this little book and it's going to be up to me to answer the question "Why?" or "What's in it for me?"

I went through the usual summary of the audience and purpose of the book. Things like:

- What will the book be good for?
- What the reader will get out of this book?
- What precisely did I want to achieve, and why should you be interested?
- Audience ... is the subject broad enough in appeal?
- And more!

What's the "And more?" Well, I thought it equally important to consider:

- What type of book do I enjoy reading myself?
- What's in it for me?

- How might writing a book help me achieve my own goals?
- And most importantly: Do I love the topic enough to invest the time and energy required to write it? After all, what's the point if it becomes work? We all have enough of that...*don't we?*

ANSWER:

I like reading anything non-fiction as long as the writer is excited about it (you can always tell) and it's important that I learn something. Something that I can apply right away.

It also has to be "bite sized" (i.e. easy to read) and I have to be able to consume it in small portions without getting lost. This might sound silly, but if you run your own business, I'm sure you understand how precious your time is. Okay, even if you don't own a business, I'm sure you appreciate how precious your time is.

I love something I can pick up and read 5 minutes at a time ... during a coffee break ... in the car when I've arrived for a meeting too early ... during a morning constitutional.

That's 5 minutes at a time.

Why should you read further... or, What's in it for you... or, Why should you care?

Imagine this book to be the door to my office and that you have been invited in to spend the day picking my brain... for FREE! The first thing I have to say is that you will learn enough to start viewing the advertising you see on a day to day basis in a different light. Second, I will speak in generalities and much of what I have to say may be oversimplified, so forgive me!

Also, I don't pretend to have an expertise on everything advertising. I will speak to what is proven to work in print advertising and what continues to produce results. I'm not a believer that advertising is about being hugely creative. I believe in advertising that works - and works hard, whether it's:

- Getting a prospect to call or e-mail

- Reminding a reader what we stand for

- Making a sale

- Getting read

- Just getting noticed

GET NOTICED

A "How-To" Guide to
SPECTACULAR Advertising!

Foreword

"What can I write about that would really help out small business owners?" Jamie said to me when he started this resolution to write.

Now, here's my perpetually enthusiastic business partner and husband with a huge wealth and variety of experiences behind him. Experienced in solving a multitude of advertising and creative issues, serving/selling varied industries and products, and yet he can't find anything to talk about?

Definitely a first.

"Jamie, you're an expert in dealing with people," I said. "You've brought large committees and boards together in solving advertising problems. You've seen individuals hugely invested in advertising solutions that didn't work, and yet

12   © Hardie & Co. - All rights reserved   www.hardieandcompany.com

you've managed to create wonderful solutions WITH them. And, you do it with inspiration, facts, and enthusiasm that's infectious!"

"So?"

"So write about the process. You know - how do you design by committee, get others thinking like in mind, and still get efforts that work -- and work hard. Why "Branding" is the soul of a dream solution and more than just a pretty logo? What makes an ad get read? What did the wonderful ad giants of the past find, and what continues to work for us today? What jewels have you gleaned from them, and why do they work so well?"

"Go on..."

"Our clients come to us from different places, with different needs, and you always have them leave a brain-storming session or seminar so excited and reeling from the great experience they've just had. Feeling part of a process somewhat bigger than themselves."

"People don't have the same knowledge you take for granted, Jamie! These are valuable tools that people can use to create their own efforts. Efforts that really work!"

"And YES, Jamie, use the word FREE some place along the way."

[signature]

Sydney Hardie
Partner, Hardie & Co.

P.S. Thanks to Jamie, I too, am brain-washed to always use a post-script.

P.P.S.. Be prepared to learn the tools that will *launch* your advertising to the next level!

Preface

$$\Big(\ \text{Recipes for Spectacular Advertising - that gets read!}\ \Big)$$

IDEAS AND CREATIVITY. BUSINESSES NEED BOTH, PERIOD.

Without creative new ideas and an understanding of how advertising influences us, our designs, no matter how pretty, will fail. We *must* understand the power ideas have. Power to transform a business' advertising efforts from lackluster, to efforts infused with enthusiasm and purpose — demanding they *get read!*

We are all purveyors of new business ideas, and we all have to understand the value we bring to what we do. So, I will also provide you with ways to communicate your ideas, sell your products and services effectively — ideally making you a happy and motivated sales person.

"That's right, sales!"

How many of you would have bought this book if you knew that I wanted to transform you into a sales person? You want to learn how to make your ads better, to convey your company's personality in a wonderfully designed effort, and to grow your bottom line, right?

Well, I always tell people that I'm not a salesman, but isn't sales what graphic design/communication is all about? Don't we want people to read what we've designed? Don't we want people to take some kind of action? Call us, respond to our e-mail, or come to our event?

Yes. We are talking about Visual Sales.

Whether you're looking for a new idea for a brochure, an ad in a trade publication, or getting someone to answer your e-mail, you are in the business of getting read.

The advertising giant, **David Ogilvy,** understood how ideas can jump-start organizations and people, as well as how to incorporate new ideas while remaining true to your organization's brand or mission statement, or vision for the marketplace. Whatever your needs are, you also need to get read. With this in mind, I hope that you take advantage of this book as a great resource.

Cheers,

Jamie

Partner, Hardie & Co.

P.S. I hope this book gets earmarked and well worn, after all, that's when *I* know I have found a great resource.

And, ultimately, that is why I've written this book.

My Exact Intention for Creating This Book – A Focus Statement

{
To create an easy, useful, and powerful tool that will help anyone create unique, personable, and appealing advertising that gets read... and sells!
}

~ Jamie Hardie, 2006
Hardie & Co... Advertising Design

 © Hardie & Co. - All rights reserved   www.hardieandcompany.com

-1-

First Off:
What Are We Talking About?

Advertising, Marketing & Public Relations

Let's take a moment to clarify/define advertising, marketing and public relations, since they are often confused, or painted with the same brush.

Marketing

Marketing is the act of getting your product or service to people, and where to sell your product or service is the job of marketers. Bringing your product or service to market, and focusing on the perception the general public has of your brand is also the job of a marketer.

© Hardie & Co. - All rights reserved   www.hardieandcompany.com   19

Public Relations

Public Relations is an effort aimed at promoting the "good name" of your business. For example: sending out a press release or news release about your business is a public relations tactic. However, it doesn't directly motivate people to buy your product or direct them to you.

Advertising

Unlike marketing and public relations, advertising refers our attempts to sell to a specific target. We want to reach a prospect / potential buyer and urge them to buy, or act.

To do this, they must know:
• Who you are
• What you sell
• Where you are
• Why they should buy from you and not one of your competitors

What Exactly is Advertising?

Albert Lasker (1880 - 1952) made more money in advertising than anyone!

Lasker was obsessed with this very question: "What *exactly* is advertising?"

He asked everyone he knew and I'm sure heard a multitude of definitions... none of which satisfied him.

Until he met a former "Canadian Mountie" turned copy-writer named John E. Kennedy.

The mustachioed Canadian Mountie, John Kennedy, defined advertising as: "Salesmanship in print."

That is - advertising should:

• Give potential customers reasons why they should buy your product

• Tell why your product is better than a competitor's.

This satisfied Lasker's search, and they began working together... to great effect, and grew to become the biggest advertising agency in the world, just before the end of the Second World War.

© Hardie & Co. - All rights reserved

So if you come away remembering only one definition, make it this one:

"Advertising is Salesmanship in Print!"

Most will agree that this is still the best definition around.

And Yes! It is worth repeating.

"Advertising is Salesmanship in Print!"

 © Hardie & Co. - All rights reserved   www.hardieandcompany.com

-2-

"A Big Fat Lie"

I f you listen to some people today, you could easily be led to believe, by all the negative information and discouraging stories, that older philosophies which made the men and women in the early days of the advertising industry successful don't apply in today's world.

Not True.

Now more than ever we are in a time when good, well considered advertising and copy is the exception, not the rule. Everyone has a computer with some type of desktop publishing software, and often a pretty picture is mistaken for a good advertising effort.

So what makes a good ad? And how do I make one?

Don't worry, we'll get to that, but for now, let me take a moment to explain why there's still so much poor advertising around.

In my opinion, agency people often (not always) focus on brokering the advertising space, or leave their stunning and well crafted efforts for their larger clients. This is understandable, since it's far more exciting than making advertisements for newspapers and magazines promoting smaller clients/products. It's more lucrative, too!

In my experience, small businesses often:

• Find ad agencies too expensive. Heck, even larger businesses want to see some return on investment, but still find agencies prohibitively expensive.

• Need more focus on sales and getting a response than longer term marketing issues (i.e. brand recognition isn't as important as making a sale).

 © Hardie & Co. - All rights reserved   www.hardieandcompany.com

I.E.

1st and 2nd tier brands like *PEPSI* or *NIKE* often can win attention just on the strength of their logo alone. They don't have to demonstrate the benefits of using a product to a potential consumer. They just have to remind people that they are there.

THAT'S A POWERFUL BRAND!

Today, it is nearly impossible for a small business to find an affordable advertising agency, and a good ad piece that works hard to sell your product or service is sometimes just as elusive. This holds true for even the not-so-small businesses as well.

So What Can I Do?

Well, you could try hunting down a retired ad man or copywriter who knows how to pull together a half decent print ad. Or you could try throwing your work to a graphic designer, who will invent a visually stunning ad., but possibly without knowing what works or why.

The silly thing is that there are practically infallible formulas for advertisements that grab a potential customer's attention and don't let it go until the message is heard.

Once you know these "secrets" (I call them secrets because they're so seldom used) it's like discovering a whole new, virtually untapped, powerful resource.

"But if these guidelines are so straightforward, why don't people use them more often?"

Good question.

You also have to stop and wonder...

How can any business afford to advertise and not see a concrete return on their investment? (More importantly how can you?)

How can I get good printed advertising without paying agency-sized fees?

More good questions.

I know, you want answers. Don't worry - they're coming soon. To quote master salesman, circus owner, and business man P.T. Barnum:

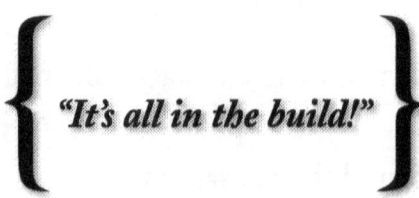

"It's all in the build!"

26   © Hardie & Co. - All rights reserved   www.hardieandcompany.com

-3-

Are You Strange?

My dad is a very opinionated (who's father isn't) 76 year old. He often talks about how good things were, and how his generation lived in simpler times and had fewer choices.

I love... *LOVE* what I do, and to me the increasing rate of change and choices means an opportunity to take on ever changing problems, solve them, and learn something along the way. I have the greatest job!

Sorry, "we" have the greatest job.

However, my dad is right about one thing: his generation did have fewer choices in the marketplace.

Today, your choices are almost limitless, and you can find a variation of a product to suite any taste, with any option you can imagine... including the kitchen sink!

Let's take refrigerators as an example:
In my father's day, most refrigerators came in two standard styles, and choice was either white, harvest gold, avocado or brown, and now the choices are virtually limitless.

1950	TODAY
Harvest Gold, White, Avocado, Brown	Unlimited colours, stainless steel
Freezer on top	Ice makers, water dispensers, wine coolers
3 main brand names	Freezer on top, side or bottom
	Hundreds of brands to choose from etc, etc.

What's my point? (*I Only...*)

We are now in a world with a mind boggling number of choices across virtually every category of products, and yet beyond traits like "value" & "service," people still have a hard time distinguishing their product or service in the marketplace.

Finding YOUR Difference!

I can't tell you how many times I've heard people say *"I only* sell widgets and lots of people sell widgets..."

What?!

I admit it, I have a problem with the words "I only..." Even saying it to myself seems to suck the wind out of my sails.

Try it.

"I only do... the housework"

"I only sell... widgets"

"I only provide..."

Not very inspiring, eh?

N.B.
The word inspiration comes from The Greek term "spiring" or "spiration" meaning "God-breathed," or "the product of the creative breath of God."

Don't worry, I'm not going to burst into prayer, but you have to admit, the imagery is powerful.

"*I only*" is <u>NOT</u> very Inspiring

Unique (*Only I...*)

"Unique". Now there's a word that is much easier to get excited about.... inspired about.

This is a huge word - and in today's super competitive market, there are fewer questions that are more important for a business to answer than this one:

How are you Unique?

How is my *company* unique?

How is my *product* unique?

How am *I* unique?

Take some time to answer these questions.

Answer them well, and you could find a key element that catapults your product from "one of many" to "the only one like it."

{
"You do not merely want to be considered the best of the best, you want to be considered the only one who does what you do."

~ Jerry Garcia, Grateful Dead
}

A hard thing to do maybe, but still a great GREAT goal!

And answering these questions **WILL** change:

• The imagery you use

• The wording you use in your ads/promotions

• How you position yourself

• Maybe even how you dress

Example: *Plant Products Co... Ltd.* is the nation's leading supplier of fertilizer, pesticides, biological pest control, substrates and seeds to ornamental and vegetable greenhouse growers, nurseries and the specialty agriculture sectors.

So, even while they mean business, they're *unique* in that they position themselves as true partners who aren't afraid to jump in and get their hands dirty to solve a problem.

This means gone is the traditional shirt and tie, and in comes a denim button down complete with rolled up sleeves.

A simple distinction, but an important one.

Are you *Strange* enough?

Have fun! Go too far! Be... ***Outrageous***!

Outrageous can be a good thing. At worst it is a memorable thing.

{ *"I don't care what they write about me, as long as they write about me!"* }

~ P.T. Barnum

Unique also means:

"When everyone zigs, it's time to ZAG!"

-4-

Revealing a Big Secret

Visual Branding

Design. It's not an easy thing to define, and defining great design is even harder. It would be nice to say that exceptional design is timeless, but the best we can agree on is that excellent designs may have a longer shelf life than not-so-excellent design.

Design a Taste

Design, like taste, is very much a subjective thing. And sometimes an advertising effort that's broad in appeal isn't effective at conveying a message, or selling a product or service.

© Hardie & Co. - All rights reserved

So how do we gauge or do good work if we can't easily define it?

What are the important things for us to consider in all this?

Well, I can't speak for the 1st tier brands of the world (the *Pepsis*, *General Electrics.* and *Apples* of the world), but I can give you some insights into what works for almost everyone else!

Here it is

Okay, we all know that relationships are very important, so what's the big secret?

And...

Are you ready?

Are you really paying attention?

Wait for it...

"People are Everything!"

YES. That's my big design secret weapon.
Are you surprised?

People *are* the source of everything. They buy our product or service. They make up all aspects of our business, from concept to delivery.

Our business is about relationships and must, above all else, *be personable*. Now, by personable I don't mean that we are insincere social butterflies, flitting around with an ear-to-ear grin.

I mean that our company must convey a personality consistent with the image we want to convey (ideally) and congruent with the personality of the people and products of our company.

So, when I talk about **brand**, I am not merely referring to the pretty logo that we spent so much time, and possibly a great deal of money, creating. No, our brand is *so* much more.

Logos are great, and for those larger brands whose logos are widely recognized and immediately convey to us wondrous feelings and visions of something more than the written copy of the ad... *congratulations!*

NOTE: Try and put a price on something like that!

– That's *powerful!*

No, when I talk about Brand, I'm referring to a much broader visual language. One that provides something more than just a pretty backdrop for copy.

It's Alive!... ALIVE!

Branding a Personality

Close your eyes. Think about your product or company. Now, envision the ideal ambassador for your effort, product, service or company. Really try and picture the *perfect person* to represent you, a true reflection of what and how you want to be seen.

Is He Alive Yet?

What personality traits would he/she have? Would he/she be;

- Energetic
- Powerful

- Enthusiastic
- Conservative

- Trustworthy
- Refined

- Steadfast
- Dependable

- Supportive
- Direct

- Resourceful
- Fun-loving
- Sincere
- Etc...

So remember "personality traits."

Would he dress

- All business - Suit and Tie

- Business Casual

- Casual

- Sleeves rolled up and ready to jump in and lend a hand (like at Plant Products Co... Ltd.).

"But I sell widgets at a good price. My customers aren't interested in **personality** - they're only interested in quality, service and price."

Wrong.

Although, all these things do matter, and matter a great deal, people do business with **people** they have a relationship with and trust.

Start a "Cult!"

I am a "Parrot Head" (a Jimmy Buffet fan), and as such I would say that to call Jimmy a musician would be a huge understatement.

Jimmy and his music have come to represent a way of life: A search for the endless summer, the perfect moment on the perfect beach, in the perfect beach town.

Jimmy isn't just a musician, he's the leader of a cult. A group of like-minded individuals, impassioned to find a life free of the stresses of city life, looking for a permanent vacation... in search of... *Margaritaville!*

Wouldn't it be great to create and develop your own unique brand into a cult?

Conclusion:

As every person is unique, so is every product, service and business. You just have to dig a little deeper to uncover that "jewel" that makes you unique, and polish it to a brilliant shine.

What could be more powerful? *Nothing!*

"Be Unique, Be Different... and let it show in everything you do!"

From Personality to Design

Now that we have a clear understanding of our personality, how is it reflected in the design of our advertising brochure or promotional efforts?

Here, we'll ask a few questions, and soon you'll not only be evaluating your competitors' efforts, but seeing ways that you can make your efforts stand apart.

That's a Promise!

I'll start by asking a few questions (don't worry, you'll see where I'm going soon enough, and I'll end the chapter with some case studies).

What images might you pick if you wanted to suggest *trust?*

a) a laser

b) a huge oak tree

c) a fire

d) an immovable boulder or rock

ANSWER: **b) a huge oak tree** *and/or* **d) an immovable boulder or rock**

© Hardie & Co. - All rights reserved

Now using the same options from above, choose which one we would use to convey *precision* or *detail-oriented*

ANSWER: **a) a laser**, right?

How about *change*?

ANSWER: **c) a fire**, perhaps?

To some degree, most of us have learned to equate certain elements (images, colours etc.) with certain traits and this association can form basic elements for consideration in the designing of our efforts.

Now let's apply the same thinking to typography. Which seems more congruent;

God

or

God

Excellence

or

EXCELLENCE

© Hardie & Co. - All rights reserved
www.hardieandcompany.com

Do you see where I'm going? Good. Now let's do the same with colour. When trying to convey a feeling, or idea;

Trust - you might want to use cooler, earthy tones, like a navy blue, brown or burgundy, neutral taupe and green (think of that old oak tree...)

Freedom - colours that invoke a feeling of airiness or expansiveness, such as sky blue, or sunny yellow or a nice bright orange

Youth - energetic brights, maybe pastels, but with more colour - pink, bright green, aqua or turquoise

Excitement - hot, vibrant colours in their purer form, as in bright reds, purple, orange

© Hardie & Co. - All rights reserved

Here are a few Case Studies to peruse.

Rosseau Lake College
MEDIA KIT

- **Tried, Trusted, and True =**
  earthy warm neutrals

- **Adventuresome Spirit =**
  active outdoor photos

- **Transformation =**
  wave imagery & *scripty* font

42   © Hardie & Co. - All rights reserved   www.hardieandcompany.com

IE: MONEY
POCKET FOLDER, LETTERHEAD & AD

- **Trusted Business** = traditional business
  picture with an intentionally straight forward layout

© Hardie & Co. - All rights reserved   www.hardieandcompany.com

Canadian Mental Health Association-Peel Branch
REVISITED LOGO

- **Enthusiasm, Health Focus =**
  energetic colour

- **Optimism and Diversity =**
  smiling people of varying ages and races

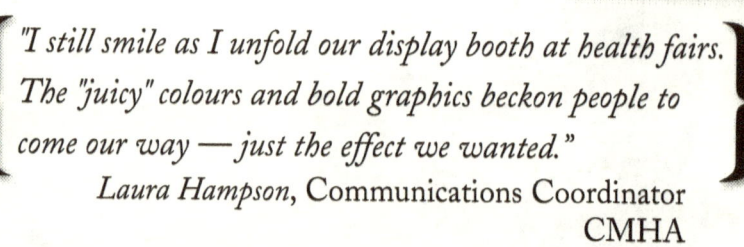

{ *"I still smile as I unfold our display booth at health fairs. The "juicy" colours and bold graphics beckon people to come our way — just the effect we wanted."*
Laura Hampson, Communications Coordinator
CMHA }

Again, have a look at brochures and advertisements around you. Better yet, take the time now to stop and consider your own visual communications. Are you conveying the visual brand that's right for you? Can you see it in the:

- *Typography*
- *Colour*
- Content of your *photography*
- Style of your *illustration*
- *Words* you choose
- *Fonts* you choose

© Hardie & Co. - All rights reserved

Plant Products Ltd.
DISPLAY PANNEL, POSTERS, BROCHURE, LOGO

- **Technical Excellence =**
  fine white lined grid pattern, all contained within a crisp white banner at the top and bottom.

Replace With COLOUR INSERT

Canadian Cancer Society
ANI

t-f   l

- photography; diverse group of individuals, jigsaw puzzle element.

- **Res**
  & pi

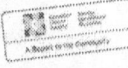

York Support Services Network
CORPORATE BROCHURE, DISPLAY BOOTH

- **Renewal** = warm spring colour palette
- **Transformation** = spring colour palette & wave motif
- *** Note** = cubes were added to help marry with the existing logo

Replace With COLOUR INSERT

Richards-Wilcox
BOOKLET

- **History/Tradition** = green & autumn orange
  a font style based on the classic artist Cezanne's handwriting,
- **Modern Engineering** = ghosted back grid pattern

© Hardie & Co. - All rights reserved

Firestorm Custom Marine
BROCHURE

- **Hi Tech =**
  keylines as
  graph-like
  element

- **Uber Cool** = pictures of boats and the
  people enjoying them

- **Custom** = logo, font treatment
  & flame

Supportive Housing in Peel
ANNUAL REPORT

- **Nurturing** = visual elements of nature
... throughout, prodominently green colour scheme

Canadian Mental Health Association
FLASH PRESENTATION

- **Approchable** = warm friendly faces "regular Joe" hand-written type face
- **Trustworthy** = softer antiqued boarder, earthy neutral colours, home "photo album" look to inset photographs.

-5-

A Design Book this Ain't ...or Maybe It Is?

No book can be all things to all people, and creating a "How To" book on design was not my intention. I'm interested in providing a great... no, a *outstanding* little resource for small business advertising.

Advertising that works hard, and gets read. I'll touch on some more basic principals of design, but I'll be speaking in generalities, so you'll have to forgive me.

Designers often think of copy as a design element to play with in order to make a pretty picture.

 © Hardie & Co. - All rights reserved

You won't find me encouraging you to do that here, but design is a piece of the puzzle and can move a well written ad from great to spectacular.

...and it can capture your prospects' attention (or repulse them)

...and can get your message read (or not)

...and can convey your totally unique and butt-kicking branded personality (or not)

Errr... okay, maybe design is the soul of a great effort after all!

We must also realize that design is the biggest differentiator between products in the marketplace. A spectacular design "captures" potential customers and immediately sets you apart from the crowd as unique.

Building a Better Ad

For arguments' sake, let's keep it simple and focus on creating layouts that follow the natural order of how we look at things:

1st - illustration or feature photograph. Ideally, showing the benefits one would get from using your product.

2nd - headline under image

3rd - copy under headline

4th - contact info and logo last

If it's powerful enough, I like to place a "Benefit" headline at the top and a teaser sub-head (one that invokes curiosity to read further) below the image. Just know that when you do this, you're making your viewer work just a little harder to read your ad.

My Design Recipe for Ads (a Summary)

To start, take lots of time and craft a glorious headline, one that answers the question "what's in it for me?" and/or gets the reader *really* curious.

Add - One bold photograph or illustration that reinforces the benefit to a consumer of using your product or service.

Mix in - a healthy amount of unique personality (branding).

Top with - contact information and a clear call to action that encourages a prospect to call you sooner, rather than later.

* Usually no salt or <u>huge</u> logo required! And don't worry, we'll touch on these points in a little more detail in "What 'They' Knew," so read on, intrepid one.

© Hardie & Co. - All rights reserved

Here are some examples that were made with consideration to this recipe.

With an appealing photo, intriguing headline, and a terrific offer, this ad - in a senior's magazine, garnered a 12% (26,000 responses) response for the client, a huge improvement on the usual .05% rate that's expected from a magazine ad.

BELOW: Bold photos, big benefit statements, plenty of personality, and clear and concise contact information.

Multiple benefits are highlighted in this ad - along with impressive photography - in order to attract students from as far away as Saudi Arabia. Just imagine how powerful a benefit picture of the Toronto Canada waterfront is, to someone from an arid climate?

© Hardie & Co. - All rights reserved

Nobody wants their romantic holiday ruined by a little arthritis! Again, showing people enjoying the benefit of the product is always a great way to go.
IE: RUB A535 gives the freedom to move (even dance) without pain.

Use a little humour to address a potentially embarrassing topic, because we can all relate to the occasional indulgences that may backfire on us (no pun intended!)

© Hardie & Co. - All rights reserved

TOUR the FANTASTIC Facilities!

"A Holiday... Everyday... Thanks Dyan!"

Sandy Cove Acres - Innisfil

A *Vibrant* community for those with a *Zest* for living!

The premier Adult Community in Ontario awaits your arrival. Filled with warm, friendly and generous people, beautiful picturesque neighbourhoods and activities for every tastes, Sandy Cove Acres is the ideal community for you.

If you enjoy; arts & crafts, swimming, golfing, reading, woodworking, day trips, dancing, cards, darts and meeting new people - CALL ME and let me be your expert resource for helping you find your perfect retirement home!

"Lately, I've found it very difficult to get good service, anywhere! But Dyan took the time to listen to our needs and wants, then looked deeply to find the place that was just perfect for us!"
Eugene Hardie,
Sandy Cove resident

Experiences...

Convenience...

Comfort...

...and More!

$78,800 2bdrms, 1.5 bth Argus Model Beautiful Treed Lot! LvgRm, FamRm, heated Sunrm. Bright Kitch. w/side door. Many upgrades include; shingled roof, vinyl siding, carpeting and tile. **PRIVACY PLUS!!**

$119,900 2 bdrm Site Built Monaco 1 1,350 s.f. open concept. LvgRm w/bay wndw, gas frpl w/mantle. Fam rm w/patio drs to deck & parkland. Mstr Bdrm w/ 3 pc ensuite. & walk-in closet. Shingled roof. drywall interior, concrete foundation.

MANY MORE HOMES AVAILABLE!

Walk the Shores of Beautiful Lake Simcoe!

Call me!

Dyan Gundert, Sales Rep.

Your Sandy Cove Resource

(24 Hour Pager) 705-722-7100 • Cell: 705-739-3056 Toronto Line 1-416-362-7100

RE/MAX®
Chay Realty Inc.

© Hardie & Co. - All rights reserved   www.hardieandcompany.com

© Hardie & Co. - All rights reserved   www.hardieandcompany.com   59

"The Lazy Creatures of Habit — We All Live With!"

We all have this lazy pair of things hanging around that we call our eyes. Our eyes have been trained to work a certain way and no matter what we do, they will continue to work in this specific and very predictable way. Our eyes are sluggish creatures of habit that:

- Read from left to right
- Read words by their shape
  (silhouette and not letter by letter)
- Are attracted to areas of high contrast
  (i.e.: light/dark vs. tone on tone)
- And tire easily

Since we know this, we want to know how to lay out a page so our "lazy friends" get all the information we want them to, quickly and easily. After all, we don't want to tire/stress our potential customers' eyes before they get our message.

We can't sell anything to anyone if we don't get read.

So, how do we make reading our ads this easy? How do we actually pull a reader in? What are the confirmed mechanics that help us accomplish this?

Use These Tools to Avoid The "Pitfalls" That Keep Your Ad From Getting Read!

- Use fonts that are easily read (*century, caslon, baskerville*).

- Use multiple columns rather than one wide column.

- Use columns no more than 30 – 40 characters wide.

- Make sure your copy is more important than your illustrations.

- Start the first paragraph with a drop capital to pull a reader into the body copy.

- Set type black on white or dark on light, not white copy on black or dark ground.

- Reversed out copy (i.e.: white type on black) is difficult to read, so keep it to a minimum. In the words of Albert Lasker, head (for 44 years) of *Lord & Thomas*, the largest agency in the world, "If it was natural to read that way, the New York Times would be printed that way."

- Think small - small sentences, short words, short paragraphs.

- Bite-sized copy gives more visual breaks (rest for the eyes) and also allows readers more opportunities to "jump in," or rather, more opportunities to have something of interest jump out and "grab" their attention.

-6-

What "They" Knew

The great ad men of the past didn't focus on fancy graphics and visual tricks, unless they worked and proved themselves valuable.

Ads were built around good copy writing, research, and tracking the results an effort pulled.

They understood the power in knowing what worked and why, so they paid close attention.

They all did. Albert Lasker 1880-1952 (who ran *Lord & Thomas*) did. So did Stanley Resor 1879-1962 (J. Walter Thompson), Raymond Rubicam (*Young & Rubicam*), Claude C. Hopkins 1866-1932, (ad man and author of the advertising classic "*Scientific Advertising*") and more recently

David Ogilvy (Founder of *Ogilvy & Mather*)

NOTE: David Ogilvy started out as a researcher before he became a copy writer.

In this section, we'll learn from them: What exactly they found in copy writing and layout that worked best and what has continued to work for us today.

So read on for a *boat load* of their sure-fire tips that you can apply right away.

Remember: OLD ≠ USELESS

{ *"On average, five times as many people read the headlines as read the body copy. It follows that unless your headline sells your products, you have wasted 90% of your money."* }

~ David Ogilvy,
Ogilvy on Advertising, Pan Books Ltd. 1983

Headlines

If anything in your ad gets read, it'll be the headline, *so have one*. Most people still never read beyond the headline of your ad, so make sure you:

- Have a headline! (remember, according to David Ogilvy, it's 90¢ of your advertising dollar!)

- Promise a benefit (like whiter teeth, freedom from pain, juicier hamburgers, the best vacation ever...)

- Include your name (you don't want to plant a seed, and then have prospects go somewhere else to buy. You don't want to be advertising for someone else, do you?)

- Make it easy to read (i.e.: upper and lower case, not all capitals, and use a serif font like caslon, etc...)

- HEADLINES ALL IN CAPITAL LETTERS ARE HARD TO READ. (see what I mean)

- Put it in quotation marks (quotes get a higher readership)

- Tell or suggest a story

- Make it newsworthy

- Get your readers curious

Get your creative juices flowing by reading these headlines:

"$1.00 Will Bring to You - The Secret of Youthful Beauty!"

"Amazing New Method Improves Skin Beauty Overnight!"

"Why America Wins Olympics"

"Distinguished Committee Launches New Soap Discovery"

"In HOLLYWOOD they advise this way to keep that school girl complexion"

© Hardie & Co. - All rights reserved

"Get Through the Winter without a Cold"

"How to Care for the Skin? Let this Well-Known Physician Answer..."

"How Dare You Mistreat Your Complexion When it is so Easy to use this Palmolive Daily Care?"

"Good Health and Pure Soap – The Simple Formula for a Beautiful Skin"

"Down from Canada Came Tales of a Wonderful Beverage"

"Woodbury Soap – The Skin you Love to Touch"

"Should You Give Your Garage Door a Closer Look?"

"They Laughed When I Sat Down at the Piano. But When I Started to Play!"

"Richards-Wilcox's Secrets Revealed! At Last! Dealers have a Resource to Help Realize Higher Profits!"

Illustration and Photography

Truth in advertising is a great thing. Consider this when choosing imagery to go in your ad. A photograph rings truer and is more trusted than an illustration, so when in doubt, use a photo.

The hardest working photographs and illustrations:

- Show a benefit in action and /or reinforces your headline.
- Get a viewer curious and gets them to want to read/learn more (suggests a story). Harold Rudolph called this "story appeal."
- Are a resource and give the reader helpful information.
- Are specific.

For example, if you're selling speed boats, never use an illustration of a boat. Use a photograph. Don't show a picture of a boat at the dock when you can show it racing along in open water. Show your ideal customer enjoying the featured benefits of your product in all the glory you can muster.

So if you're trying to sell speed boats, show a shot of your boat, going full bore on a gorgeous sunny day with its owner and his perfect family all smiling "ear to ear!"

- Illustrate the benefit by showing before and after pictures.

- Show the end result or the "You Get...". Even images of the freshest ingredients (tomatoes, red peppers, etc.) don't get as good a response as that of the steaming hot, finished pizza, provided you are selling pizza, and not vegetables.

N.B.

David Ogilvy found that even when you advertise the individual products for use in cooking, you attract more readers if you show a photograph of the finished dish rather than the ingredients.

Body Copy

I always hear people say that lots of copy doesn't work, so don't use too much, or the "Less is More" philosophy.

Not necessarily.

It's true that it's often difficult to get people to read a large amount of copy (thanks to those lazy creatures of habit). But if you do get read, long copy gives you the opportunity to do more selling and push your message in deeper.

REMEMBER: *If you want people to read your text, make it readable!*

David Ogilvy noted that Louis Engel of Merrill Lynch wrote a single page ad that had 6,540 words — WOW!

But did it work?

Yes: It was placed in the back of the *New York Times* and pulled 10,000 responses, even without a coupon!

- People have to be interested in the kind of product/service you're advertising.

- Make people want to read it; your copy should be written in everyday language, as if you're having a conversation with a friend.

- Tell readers what your products or service will do for them, and be specific; don't say "pet" if you can say "dog," don't say "dog" if you can say "Retriever," and don't just say "Retriever" if you can say "my best friend and Golden Retriever named Molly."

- Use testimonials. They make you more credible. Testimonials = *Trust*

- Consumers also like freebies, discounts, contests and special offers. These answer the question "What's in it for me?"

- If you are able, consider including the price. Do you recall the expression "If you have to ask, you probably can't afford it."?

- Tell a story with your copy

- **P.S.** Postscripts get read, so summarize key points you want remembered and the action you want people to take.

A last consideration by David Ogilvy from his book, *Ogilvy on Advertising*:

"I am sometimes attacked for imposing 'rules'. Nothing could be further from the truth. I hate rules. All I do is report how consumers react to different stimuli. I may say to an art director 'research suggests that if you set the copy in black type on a white ground, more people will read it than if you set it in white type on a black background.' A hint, perhaps, but scarcely a rule."

© Hardie & Co. - All rights reserved

N.B.

If you liked this section and want to learn more... way more.... you *have to read these great books:* Joe Vitalie's book, ***AMA Complete Guide to Small Business Advertising,*** NTC Business Books ©1995 and David Ogilvy's, ***Ogilvy On Advertising***, PAN Book Ltd. © 1983.

72   © Hardie & Co. - All rights reserved   www.hardieandcompany.com

Classic Ads Worth a Look!

Here's a great old example of telling a story with the copy, done by the venerable old expert, John Caples, in 1925

People respond better to stories than simply facts and statements, so tell the story of a client who has bought your product or used your service... and benefitted.

 © Hardie & Co. - All rights reserved www.hardieandcompany.com

Here's some more classic examples from way, way back. Can you see this stuff in practice?

Asking "Who Else..." makes for a great start to a headline.

© Hardie & Co. - All rights reserved   www.hardieandcompany.com   75

Mrs. James J. Davis, wife of the Secretary of Labor and Senator-elect from Pennsylvania, presided as chairman of the Committee of 17.

Section of the Committee of 17 watch revolutionary new soap tested at Ritz Hotel. (Left to right) Dr. McGowan, Antoinette Donnelly, Suzanne Pollard Boatwright (Mrs. Herbert Lee Boatwright, Jr.), Miss Edgerton and Ex-Governor Ross.

Mary Roberts Rinehart, member of the Committee of 17 and famed for her exceedingly successful novels, the most recent of which is "The Door."

Distinguished Committee of 17 Launches New Soap Discovery

Mrs. James J. Davis, Mrs. Cecil B. deMille, Ethel Barrymore, Anne Morgan, in group to judge new soap for fine fabrics

Ethel Barrymore, of the Committee of 17, America's most famous actress. She and her daughter are appearing together in "Scarlet Sister Mary."

A TINY bead of soap, no larger than a pinhead, yet it holds the secret of 20% longer wear for silk stockings! Science proved that recently to the entire satisfaction of the Committee of 17, a group of distinguished women who met at the Ritz Hotel to give "the woman's viewpoint" on this revolutionary new soap that promises to upset utterly all previous conceptions of how silks and fine fabrics should be washed.

Watch soap tests at Ritz

Social leaders, home economics consultants, the wife of a distinguished cabinet member, eminent university authorities . . . women representative of every type of American femininity . . . the Committee of 17 heard silk experts tell how modern hasty washbowl laundering demanded an entirely different kind of soap from flakes or granules. How silks and woolens, to give longer wear, should be washed in a soap that would dissolve instantly—work in water as cool as 81° F. and rinse away completely.

Could such a soap be made? Silk experts said "yes." And before the watching committee they tested a revolutionary new soap, called "Palmolive Beads." Tiny, jade green beads of soap that dissolved like a flash. Cleansed in water 20 degrees cooler than ordinary soaps require. And rinsed away

in water of the same low, safe temperature. Not a trace of gummy, half-dissolved soap left to spot or damage fine fabrics!

Distinguished committee approves new soap discovery

So perfectly did the new soap meet every requirement that the Committee of 17 went on record as "unanimously approving Palmolive Beads as perfect for the washing of silks, woolens and all fine fabrics."

Palmolive Beads are the first soap for fine silks ever made in the form of tiny, hollow, instant-dissolving "beads." The only fine fabric soap ever made of olive and palm oils . . . oils hitherto reserved exclusively for complexion soaps. It is for sale at all dealers at 10 cents the box. Get a box today.

Famous Silk Manufacturers

unite with Committee of 17 in endorsing Palmolive Beads

CHENEY	CORTICELLI
BOLSPROOF	KAYSER
LUXITE	PHOENIX
STEHLI	VANITY FAIR
VAN RAALTE	

They analyzed Palmolive Beads in their own laboratories. They tested them again and again in washing tests and the silks they manufacture. And now at recommend Palmolive Beads for safe washing of silks.

The Committee of 17

These hostess women — leaders representing every phase of feminine activity, from all over the United States — approved and sponsor Palmolive Beads.

MRS. JAMES J. DAVIS
Wife of Secretary of Labor.

ETHEL BARRYMORE
America's most famous actress.

ELSIE DE WOLFE
Noted authority on decoration.

ANTOINETTE DONNELLY
Chicago beauty expert.

LILLIAN EGERTON
Head of textile laboratory.

MRS. KELLOGG FAIRBANK
Famous Chicago social leader.

MRS. OLIVER HARRIMAN
New York social leader.

ANNE MORGAN
Renowned breaker of a famous father.

DR. ELLEN B. McGOWAN
Of a great eastern university.

MARY ROBERTS RINEHART
Noted fiction writer.

MRS. FRANKLIN ROOSEVELT
Wife of the Governor of New York.

NELLIE TAYLOR ROSS
Ex-Governor of Wyoming.

GAY S. WALTON
Stylist for silk manufacturer.

SUZANNE POLLARD BOATWRIGHT
(Mrs. Herbert Lee Boatwright, Jr.) Daughter of Governor of Virginia.

MRS. HANCOCK BANNING
California social leader.

MRS. CECIL B. DE MILLE
Wife of the famous director.

MME. SCHUMANN-HEINK
America's most prima donna.

PALMOLIVE BEADS

for washing fine fabrics.   *Large Box 10¢*

PALMOLIVE BEADS

Notice how much this resembles an editorial page from a newspaper? People are more interested in reading news than advertising

 © Hardie & Co. - All rights reserved   www.hardieandcompany.com

"Here's an Extra $50, Grace
—I'm making <u>real</u> money now!"

"Yes, I've been keeping it a secret until pay day came. I've been promoted with an increase of $50 a month. And the first extra money is yours. Just a little reward for urging me to study at home. The boss says my spare time training has made me a valuable man to the firm and there's more money coming soon. We're starting up easy street, Grace, thanks to you and the I. C. S.!"

Today more than ever before, money is what counts. The cost of living is mounting month by month. You can't get along on what you have been making. Somehow, you've simply got to increase your earnings.

Fortunately for you hundreds of thousands of other men have proved there is an unfailing way to do it. Train yourself for bigger work, learn to do some one thing well and employers will be glad to pay you real money for your special knowledge.

You can get the training that will prepare you for the position you want in the work you like best, whatever it may be. You can get it without sacrificing a day or a dollar from your present occupation. You can get it at home, in spare time, through the International Correspondence Schools.

It is the *business* of the I. C. S. to prepare men in just your circumstances for better positions at better pay. They have been doing it for 28 years. They have helped two million other men and women. They are training over 100,000 now. Every day many students write to tell of advancements and increased salaries already won.

You have the same chance they had. What are you going to do with it? Can you afford to let a single priceless hour pass without at least finding out what the I. C. S. can do for you? Here is all we ask—without cost, without obligating yourself in any way, simply mark and mail this coupon.

—TEAR OUT HERE—

INTERNATIONAL CORRESPONDENCE SCHOOLS
BOX   SCRANTON, PA.

Explain, without obligating me, how I can qualify for the position, or in the subject, before which I mark X.

MEN WANTED for Hazardous Journey. Small wages, bitter cold, long months of complete darkness, constant danger, safe return doubtful. Honor and recognition in case of success — Ernest Shakleton.

"It seemed as though all the men in Great Britain were determined to accompany me, the response was so overwhelming."
~ Ernest Shackleton

 © Hardie & Co. - All rights reserved   www.hardieandcompany.com

"To men who want to *Quit Work* some day"
What "man" wouldn't want to read on?

© Hardie & Co. - All rights reserved

Do You Make These Mistakes in English?

Sherwin Cody's remarkable invention has enabled more than 100,000 people to correct their mistakes in English. Only 15 minutes a day required to improve your speech and writing.

MANY persons use such expressions as "Leave them lay there" and "Mary was invited as well as myself." Still others say "between you and I" instead of "between you and me." It is astonishing how often "who" is used for "whom" and how frequently we hear such glaring mispronunciations as "for MID able," "ave NOO," and "KEW pon." Few know whether to spell certain words with one or two "c's" or "m's" or "r's" or with "ie" or "ei," and when to use commas in order to make their meaning absolutely clear. Most persons use only common words—colorless, flat, ordinary. Their speech and their letters are lifeless, monotonous, humdrum.

Why Most People Make Mistakes

What is the reason so many of us are deficient in the use of English and find our careers stunted in consequence? Why is it some cannot spell correctly and others cannot punctuate? Why do so many find themselves at a loss for words to express their meaning adequately? The reason for the deficiency is clear. Sherwin Cody discovered it in scientific tests which he gave thousands of times. Most persons do not write or speak good English simply because they never formed the habit of doing so.

What Cody Did at Gary

The formation of any habit comes only from constant practice. Shakespeare, you may be sure, never studied rules. No one who writes and speaks correctly thinks of rules when he is doing so.

Here is our mother-tongue, a language that has built up our civilization, and without which we should all still be muttering savages! Yet our schools, by wrong methods, have made it a study to be avoided—the hardest of tasks instead of the most fascinating of games! For years it has been a crying disgrace.

In that point lies the real difference between Sherwin Cody and the schools! Here is an illustration: Some years ago Mr. Cody was invited by the author of the famous Gary System of Education to teach

SHERWIN CODY

English to all upper-grade pupils in Gary, Indiana. By means of unique practice exercises Mr. Cody secured more improvement in these pupils in five weeks than previously had been obtained by similar pupils in two years under old methods. There was no guesswork about these results. They wer proved by scientific comparisons. Amazing as this improvement was, more interesting still was the fact that the children were "wild" about the study. It was like playing a game!

The basic principle of Mr. Cody's new method is habit-forming. Anyone can learn to write and speak correctly by constantly using the correct forms. But how is one to know in each case what is correct? Mr. Cody solves this problem in a simple, unique, sensible way.

100% Self-Correcting Device

Suppose he himself were standing forever at your elbow. Every time you mispronounced or misspelled a word, every time you violated correct grammatical usage, every time you used the wrong word to express what you meant, suppose pro could hear him whisper: "That is wrong, it should be thus and so." In a short time you would habitually use the correct form and the right words in speaking and writing.

If you continued to make the same mistakes over and over again, each time patiently he would tell you what was right. He would, as it were, be an everlasting mentor beside you—a mentor who would not laugh at you, but who would, on the contrary, support and help you. The 100% Self-Correcting Device does exactly this thing. It is Mr. Cody's silent voice behind you, ready to speak out whenever you commit an error. It finds your mistakes and concentrates on them You do not need to study anything you already know There are no rules to memorize.

Only 15 Minutes a Day

Nor is there very much to learn. In Mr. Cody's years of experimenting he brought to light some highly astonishing facts about English.

For instance, statistics show that a list of sixty-one words (with their repetitions) make up more than half of all our speech and letter-writing. Obviously, if one could learn to spell, use, and pronounce these words correctly, one would go far toward eliminating incorrect spelling and pronunciation.

Similarly, Mr. Cody proved that there were no more than one dozen fundamental principles of punctuation. If we mastered these principles, there would be no bugbear of punctuation to handicap us in our writing.

Finally, he discovered that twenty-five typical errors in grammar constitute nine-tenths of our everyday mistakes. When one has learned to avoid these twenty-five pitfalls, how readily one can obtain the facility of speech which denotes the person of breeding and education!

When the study of English is made so simple, it becomes clear that progress can be made in a very short time. No more than fifteen minutes a day is required. Fifteen minutes, not of study, but of fascinating practice! Mr. Cody's students do their work in any spare moment they can snatch. They do it riding to work or at home. They take fifteen minutes from the time usually spent in profitless reading or amusement. The results really are phenomenal.

Sherwin Cody has placed an excellent command of the English language within his grasp of everyone. Those who take advantage of his method gain something so priceless that it cannot be measured in terms of money. They gain a mark of breeding that cannot be erased as long as they live. They gain a facility in speech that marks them as educated people in whatever society they find themselves. They gain the self-confidence and self-respect which this ability inspires. As for material reward, certainly the importance of good English in the race for success cannot be overestimated. Surely, no one can advance far without it.

FREE — Book on English

It is impossible in this brief review to give more than a suggestion of the range of subjects covered by Mr. Cody's new method and of what his practice exercises consist. But those who are interested can find a detailed description in a fascinating little book called "How You Can Master Good English in 15 Minutes a Day." This is published by the Sherwin Cody School of English in Rochester. It can be had by anyone, free upon request. There is no obligation involved in writing for it. The book is more than a prospectus. Unquestionably, it tells one of the most interesting stories about education in English ever written.

If you are interested in learning more in detail of what Sherwin Cody can do for you, send for the book "How You Can Master Good English in 15 Minutes a Day."

Merely mail the coupon, a letter or postal card for it now. No agent will call. SHERWIN CODY SCHOOL OF ENGLISH, 8811 B. & O. Building, Rochester 4, N. Y.

SHERWIN CODY SCHOOL OF ENGLISH
8811 B & O Building, Rochester 4, N. Y.

Please send me, without obligation on my part, your new free book "How You Can Master Good English in 15 Minutes a Day." No agent will call.

Name ....

Address ....

Zone No.
CITY .... (If any)...........State...........
☐ If 30 or under, check here for Booklet A

Again, <u>very</u> editorial looking.

80   © Hardie & Co. - All rights reserved   www.hardieandcompany.com

A Beauty Secret
3,000 Years Old

The use of palm and olive oils to keep the skin fresh and smooth is nothing new, but a secret known to pretty girls since Cleopatra's time. Her Palmolive came in vessels and jars, and she had to do her own mixing. But the beautifying cleanser she achieved was the inspiration of the mild, soothing blend science produces today.

Take a lesson from Cleopatra, who kept her youthful beauty long after girlhood's days had passed. She used cosmetics to embellish and enhance her charm, just as women do today. But the foundation was a skin thoroughly and healthfully cleansed from all clogging and dangerous accumulations.

Perfected for washing faces

Palmolive is blended from the same palm and olive oils Cleopatra used—they are the mildest, most soothing ingredients science has been able to discover.

The scientific combination of these rare oils produces a smooth, creamy, lotion-like lather. Palmolive soothes and beautifies while it cleanses. It keeps the skin of the face and body beautifully soft and smooth.

The importance of thorough cleansing

It is absolutely essential to complexion beauty to wash your face thoroughly once a day. Palmolive makes this cleansing doubly beneficial by its mildness.

The profuse, creamy lather penetrates each tiny pore, removing the deposits of dirt, oil and perspiration which cause clogging and enlargement. Such cleansing is the secret of fresh, smooth skins, as results prove. It stimulates circulation, keeps the texture fine, smooth and youthful.

The woman who fears that washing will age her skin has used the wrong soap. She will change her mind once she tries Palmolive.

Don't neglect the body

Care of the complexion only begins with the face. Your neck is just as noticeable for beauty, or the lack of it. Arms and shoulders should be kept white and smooth.

Use Palmolive for bathing and these results are accomplished. It does for your body what it does for the face.

If this seems an extravagance, remember the modest price. The firm, long-wearing cake of generous size costs but ten cents.

Our price secret

If Palmolive were made in small quantities it would be a very expensive soap.

Palm and Olive oils are most costly soap ingredients, and come from overseas.

But the popularity which requires enormous production has reduced the price to that of ordinary soaps. The Palmolive factories work day and night. The rare oils are imported in such vast volume that the manufacturing costs are reduced.

Thus Palmolive, which, if priced according to quality, would cost at least 25 cents, is yours for a modest 10 cents. You can afford this greatest of all luxuries for every toilet purpose.

THE PALMOLIVE COMPANY
Milwaukee, U. S. A.

THE PALMOLIVE COMPANY OF CANADA, Limited
Toronto, Ontario
Makers of a complete line of toilet articles

Volume and efficiency produce
25-cent quality for

10c

PALMOLIVE

© Hardie & Co. - All rights reserved   www.hardieandcompany.com   81

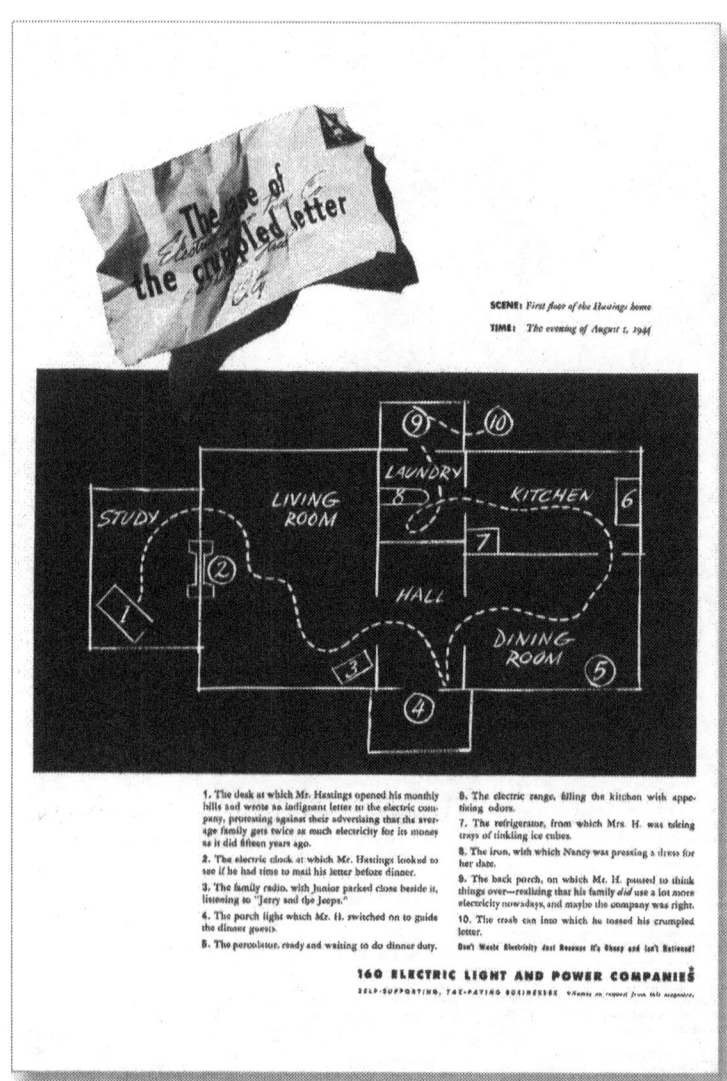

Curiosity provolking; a mystery to be solved.

© Hardie & Co. - All rights reserved
www.hardieandcompany.com

-7-

Spectacular Words - Spectacular Results

The words we use determine the type of response we get.

What?

Powerful, dramatic words make us respond in a more powerful, dramatic way.

Prove it!

Okay, say the word "*nice*" out loud.

"Nice."

Now say "*I'm tickled pink*" out loud.

Try "*okay*".

Now say "*spectacular*".

Feel the difference?

Did you smile?

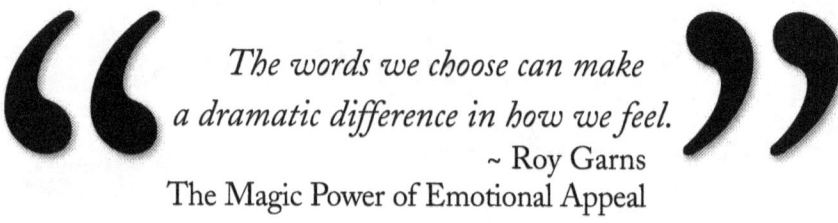

> *The words we choose can make*
> *a dramatic difference in how we feel.*
> ~ Roy Garns
> The Magic Power of Emotional Appeal

Let go of your preconceived ideas about what you do. Forget that voice that says "I can't, I'm not a designer", or "I don't know how to..." , "Don't I have to go to school for years to learn this?" "I'm not a copywriter" "I'm not a designer".

As Nike would say, "*Just Do it!*"
Just *write*!

-*8*-

Sincerity

When you think of the ad greats of the past, or even today's advertising, the word "sincerity" isn't the first, second or even in the top five words that usually come to mind.

In fact, we often think of advertising as unwanted pushy garbage that clutters our mailboxes and inboxes, radios and T.V.s, even invades the scenery outside, trying to sell us stuff that we don't want.

Some traditional copywriters and advertisers tell you that it's not important that you believe in what you are selling.

You should be able to sell anything to anyone... without

© Hardie & Co. - All rights reserved

sincerity... without guilt... without emotion.

BULL!

It may be true that a good ad man could "sell ice cream to the Eskimos" but why would he?

MONEY.

Yes, money is a great motivator, but no product or service is going to last long unless it proves itself valuable. And I, for one, would rather have the candy store tomorrow rather than a candy today (the candy store being a long term client/partner that sees us as a valuable resource that helps them solve a problem).

Wouldn't you?

If a good ad man/marketer/designer can sell a product he doesn't believe in, a book he hasn't read, or a brand company he hasn't taken the time to get to know, just think what he could do if he had a sincere belief in what he was advertising.

Insanely great ads would surely be the result.

Great ads and happy clients that buy, and buy repeatedly.

People buy a product or service because they trust in it, and

© Hardie & Co. - All rights reserved   www.hardieandcompany.com

the number one reason people don't buy is because they don't trust it will deliver on what is promised.

"Honesty Shows, Sincerity Sells!"

Or as Bruce Barton put it,

I believe the public has a sixth sense of detecting insincerity and we run a tremendous risk if we try to make other people believe in something we don't believe in. Somehow our sin will find us out.

~Bruce Barton, 1925

© Hardie & Co. - All rights reserved

One Thing We Can All Learn From the *Not For Profit* Sector

I started out as a social worker in the mental health field. I was fresh out of school, and had the wonderful opportunity to work with the *Canadian Mental Health Association* (CMHA). Saving the world, one person at a time, was my goal then. But eventually I went back to school and chose another career. And it wasn't because of the pay scale. I wanted a career with a little more freedom... a greed of another sort.

I did benefit, and greatly, by my time in the not-for-profit sector. I got to know people truly committed to helping others, powerful personalities, passionate about their industry and what they were selling.

Yes, selling.

Day in and day out these firecrackers sold people on the long term goal of mental health and ultimately a better life. Both are things we all struggle with from time to time.

Sounds like a great product to me.

As a result of my association with agency's like CMHA

Peel, Legal Aid Society of Ontario (LASO), Canadian Cancer Society (CCS), Supportive Housing in Peel (SHIP), etc., I have been fortunate enough to work with these impassioned individuals and our sincerity (both mine and theirs) showed... and sold.

When we re-branded CMHA as an energetic, passionate and healthy organization (the focus is on mental *health* as opposed to *illness*), I was pumped and totally sincere. And it showed. It showed in how both staff and clients responded to it and it continued to prove itself with an exceptionally long shelf life.

{ *"Sometimes when I consider what tremendous consequences come from little things, I am tempted to think, there are no little things."* }

~ Bruce Barton, 1925

Value in your *heart* or value in your *mind*

Okay, maybe it's not as hard to be sincere when you're promoting warm and fuzzy not-for-profits, but this still holds true with any product... that you believe in.

That belief in the value of a product can be in your mind as well as in your heart.

Church Dwight has a variety of products that many of us believe in and value because we've tried them; *Diovol, Ovol, RubA535*, etc.

When we created ads for them, I believe the fact that I have used *Diovol* (a remedy for heartburn and indigestion) allowed me to do a better job. And the results showed it. We got incredible responses - over 12% for one particular effort - in an area that typically gets a .002 to .05% response rate.

Think about it.

Everyone wants to make money for their efforts, but if you want to keep a customer, *deliver* on what you promise. People don't trust advertising and if you don't believe in what your selling or doing, how will you get anyone else excited about it?

{ *"The advertisements which persuade people to act are written by men who have an abiding respect for the intelligence of their readers, and a deep sincerity regarding the merits of the goods they have to sell."* }

~ Bruce Barton, 1925

Pulling it all Together

A Checklist:

1 First, *Find Your Unique Difference:*

Think of the "Only I..." of what you do/offer, and let it show. Dig deeper than the obvious.

In imagery, words you choose, how you position yourself, how you dress.

2 Secondly, *Be Personable*

Is your visual branding congruent with the personality you want to convey?

3 *Make your Print Ads Work Harder:*

Do you have a big beautiful photo that shows the benefit of your product in action? Is your headline powerful?* Does it state the benefit to your reader, and/or does it pique his/her curiosity?

*Remember, this is 90¢ of your advertising dollar. Make sure your copy is easily read. How can readers find you? Do you have a strong "Call to Action"?

4   *Be Sincere:*

Do you believe in the value of what you're offering? If not you better find another product or service.

5   *Follow What Works*

What is new isn't necessarily better.

What is old isn't necessarily outmoded or useless.

If you <u>must</u> choose between a pretty design & effective copy, choose the <u>effective</u>.

© Hardie & Co. - All rights reserved

About the Author

Jamie Hardie, an independent advertising and design strategist, speaker and partner of *Hardie & Company* helps a huge variety of small business and not-for-profits develop brands and produce advertising that *Gets Noticed.*

A classically trained illustrator turned "ad man" although the author of way too many ads, this is Jamie's first foray into book publishing.

Having read literally hundreds of books on advertising and effective design, his credentials are him, his experience, boundless enthusiasm and that fact that he can deliver on a promise!

© Hardie & Co. - All rights reserved
www.hardieandcompany.com

"I learned to be a copywriter by investing time and energy studying the greats of the past, (and present) and testing to find what still works!"

If you have stories to share, or if you have used any of the principals in this book and been successful, let the author know. Your example /story could be used in a future book.

Send your ideas to:

Jamie Hardie, Hardie & Co...
654 Lakelands Ave., Innisfil, ON Canada L9S 4E6
jamie@hardieandcompany.com
or visit www.hardieandcompany.com
CALL: (705)-436-5120

Bibliography... and a cool reading list

Barnum, Phineas Taylor
Selected Letters of P.T. Barnum
(Columbia University Press, NY 1983)

Barton, Bruce
The Book Nobody Knows
(The Bobbs-Merrill Co..., 1926)

Barton, Bruce
The Man Nobody Knows
(The Bobbs-Merrill Co..., 1924)

Caples, John
Tested Advertising Methods
(Englewood Cliffs, NJ. Prentice Hall, 1974)

Garn, Roy
The Magic Power of Emotional Appeal
Englewood Cliffs, NJ. Prentice Hall, 1960)

Hopkins, Claude
Scientific Advertising
Published 1923

Ogilvy, David
Confessions of an Advertising Man
(Dell Publishing Co. Inc., NY 1963)

 © Hardie & Co. - All rights reserved

Ogilvy, David
Ogilvy on Advertising
(Orbis Publishing, London 1983)

Peters, Tom
Re-Imagine! Business Excellence in a Disruptive Age
(Dorling Kindersley Limited, London, 2003)

Vitale, Joe
AMA Complete Guide to Small Business Advertising
(NTC/Contemporary Publishing Group Inc., Chicago, Illinois, 1995)

Vitale, Joe
The Seven Lost Secrets of Success
(Vista Rton, Ashland, OH., 1992

Vitale, Joe
There's a Customer Born Every Minute - P.T. Barnum's Secrets to Business Success.
(American Management Association, NY 1998

Watkins, Julian Lewis
The 100 Greatest Advertisements
(Dover Publications Inc., 1949)

© Hardie & Co. - All rights reserved   www.hardieandcompany.com

{
**For more information
on Jamie Hardie
go to:
www.hardieandcompany.com**
}

{ *"I believe hugely in advertising and blowing my own trumpet, beating the gongs, drums, etc. to attract attention to a **show**..."* }

~ P.T. Barnum

 © Hardie & Co. - All rights reserved www.hardieandcompany.com

www.ingramcontent.com/pod-product-compliance
Lightning Source LLC
Chambersburg PA
CBHW031246280526
45784CB00004B/1733